CHEROKEE MYTHOLOGY & LEGENDS

Journey To Exploring the Deities and Legendary Tales

Mythweaver Press

Copyright © 2023

All rights reserved. Without the showing prior written permission of the publisher, no portion of this book may be copied, kept in a retrieval system, or communicated in any form, whether mechanical, electronic, photocopying, recording or otherwise. This includes transmitting it in any language.

Copyright © 2023

Disclaimer

The author is solely responsible for this book's information, ideas, and opinions; they do not necessarily represent the views of any organizations, institutions, or individuals associated with the author. The author has made what they believe to be reasonable steps to make sure that the material contained in this book is accurate. However, neither the author nor the publisher makes any representations or guarantees, either stated or implied, regarding the completeness, accuracy, reliability, appropriateness, or availability of the content contained within. It is strongly recommended that readers seek assistance from relevant professionals or specialists in specific disciplines by consulting with them to acquire precise information tailored to their particular situations. The author disclaims liability for any loss, damage, or harm resulting from using the information provided in this book and any omissions or errors.

This book may reference websites, goods, services, or resources owned or operated by third parties. These references are solely offered for your convenience, and their inclusion does not indicate that we approve, sponsor, or recommend the content provided by the third party. Because the author and the publisher do not have any control over the nature, content, or availability of external websites, they cannot be held liable for any actions, decisions, or consequences resulting from using such external resources.

Forward

I would want to extend an invitation to go on a voyage that is genuinely extraordinary to those of you who are interested in unearthing ancient knowledge, who are captivated by the mysterious stories that are woven through the fabric of human life, and who are aficionados of the rich tapestry of mythology that transcends boundaries and resonates across time. Within this book's covers, we will explore the halls of myth and completely submerge ourselves in the ageless tales that have enthralled the human imagination for as long as anybody can remember. We will go through the realms of both the divine and the mortal, from the lofty heights of Mount Olympus to the maze-like depths of the underworld, from the holy riverbanks of the Ganges to the enigmatic lands inhabited by Norse gods; in short, we will explore the entirety of the multiverse.

In all of its magnificence, mythology acts as a compass that directs us through the complexities of the human experience. It is a mirror that reflects our perception of the universe and our role and embodies our collective dreams, fears, goals, and ideals. Mythology invites us to investigate the hidden aspects of our lives, whether we are more interested in the sweeping conflicts between gods and heroes or the hidden meanings in the stories of how the world was created.

Within these pages, you will encounter many pantheons and deities, each providing a distinctive perspective to examine the more expansive universe. As we delve deeper into these enthralling tales, it is essential to remember that mythology is not only a relic of the past but a living phenomenon that continues to impact our contemporary reality. Its influence can be seen in literature, art, music, and daily language. It invigorates us, sparks the fire of our imagination, and gives us a glimpse into the intricate web that is the history of humanity.

Mythology also acts as a connector, bringing together people from different cultures worldwide. It brings us together by highlighting the similarities in our experiences and the uniqueness of each of us as individuals. In the vast pantheon of mythical figures, we find examples of universal themes such as love, betrayal, heroism, and sacrifice. These themes connect with every human heart, regardless of when or where they were written.

This book is both a celebration of mythology and an invitation to go on an adventure of discovery. This is a homage to the innumerable storytellers who have ensured the survival of these myths through the ebb and flow of the sands of time by passing them down from generation to generation. It is devoted to all people interested in mythology, namely those who find comfort in the ageless stories that have shaped our world since the beginning of time and continue to do so today.

Therefore, I implore you, dear reader, to turn the page and completely submerge yourself in the enthralling delights that are still to come. Let us all come together to celebrate the mythology that brings us together that is not limited by the constraints of culture or time and imparts a feeling of awe and wonder into our everyday lives.

Your imagination will be stoked, your horizons will be expanded, and you will be reminded of the eternal power of storytelling if you allow yourself to go on this voyage into the realms of mythology. And may you emerge from these pages, like the heroes of old, changed by the insight and enchantment that mythology has to give due to what you've learned here.

TABLE OF CONTENTS

Forward

Chapter 1: Introduction

Chapter 2: Cherokee Gods
Asgaya Gigagei (God of Thunder)
Dayunsi (Creator God)

Chapter 3: Cherokee Goddess
Unelanuhi (Sun Goddess)

Chapter 4: Cherokee Creatures
Nunnehi: Travel Sprit
Jistu: Trickiest Rabbit
Ocasta

Chapter 5: Cherokee Legends
Kananesky Amaiyehi
Uktena And Ulunsuti
Corn and Medicine
Ani Hyuntikwalaski
The creation myth of the Cherokee
The First Woman
Daughter of the Sun

CHAPTER 1: INTRODUCTION

The Cherokee people are Native Americans indigenous to the Southeastern Woodlands and currently reside predominately in North Carolina and Oklahoma villages. Cherokee spiritual beliefs are maintained in common by all Cherokee people. Some of the beliefs and the tales and songs used to preserve them can be found in somewhat varying forms among the various groups that have worked to keep them alive. However, they still come together to form a coherent theological framework for the most significant part.

Traditional Cherokee cosmology includes the idea that the cosmos comprises three separate but interconnected realms. These are called the Upper, Under, and This World. The Upper World & the Under World are both considered to be the domains of the spirits. In contrast to the teachings of other religions, Cherokee spirituality does not place humans in a position of authority or dominion over the natural world, including its flora and fauna. Instead, human beings interact peacefully with the rest of the created world. The humans act as a mediator between all the planets to keep the harmony between them all intact. Plants, animals, and other aspects of the natural world and other geological structures have unique spiritual qualities and characteristics.

The foundation of Cherokee mythology is a set of beliefs concerning totemic spirits claimed to have been responsible for the creation of the universe. Also, it is believed that these spirits are the ones who initiate and deliver things like dreams, visions, signals, and a whole host of other things. The Cherokee people believed that the tiny water beetle, also known as Dayuni's, formed the original earth. They believed that the beetle descended from the heavens to the ground below. At that time, water completely encircled the Earth, and ropes were attached to the planet at all four cardinal points. As a result, the planet was suspended in space.

Following a brief period of paddling, the beetle extracted dirt from the water, and it was this mud that eventually spread out in all directions to build the earth. After witnessing the little water beetle's miracle in the sky, many other spirits were urged to travel down to earth. As a result, several different kinds of animals were dispatched to investigate it; initially, a bird was dispatched to determine how dry the ground was, and a buzzard came as a forerunner for the rest of the creatures. The Cherokee people value this origin myth highly and believe it to be true.

In Cherokee mythology, the spirits that are said to be responsible for indications, dreams, and visions are referred to as yats. Unelanuhi, the sun goddess, is considered the most crucial figure in Cherokee mythology. It is said that Unelanuhi possesses all knowledge and wisdom and is commonly regarded as the leader of the earth. After the small beetle was responsible for the creation of the earth, Unelanuhi became the king of the earth and was responsible for overseeing all of the activities that took place on it. According to urban legend, she was the one who commanded the planet to continue the human race in her name.

In Cherokee mythology, most illnesses and misfortune that befall the people are attributed to witchcraft, and there is no belief in science's role in these occurrences. It was believed that the plants that grew on Earth produced a medicine that could treat all the illnesses on Earth.

Suppose the supernatural beings that figure prominently in Cherokee mythology are left out of the conversation. In that case, the subject cannot be considered entirely. Oral literature is the primary means by which the legends and folklore of the Cherokee people are transmitted from one generation to the next; specific literature has only a small number of written examples of Cherokee storytelling.

Explore the wondrous world of Cherokee mythology, where long-forgotten stories and spiritual beliefs combine to build a complex web of traditional Native American lore. Learn about the knowledge and the magic passed down through the decades to shape the cultural heritage of the Cherokee people. Suppose you want to understand better the spiritual connection between people and the natural world. In that case, the engaging stories and rich symbolism of Cherokee mythology are excellent places to start. Immerse yourself in them. Feel the transformational force of these stories that have stood the test of time and that resonate with the unyielding spirit of the Cherokee tribe.

When you turn the pages of this book, you will be transported to a realm in which potent deities such as the Great Thunder and the Long Man rule over the elements of the natural world. Learn about the intriguing myths surrounding Uktena, the serpent of wisdom, and Selu, the corn mother who provides for her people. Please participate in the telling of tales about the eternal Ani Tsutsa, which are the ancestral spirits that the Cherokee people believe guide and protect them. As you read these compelling narratives, you will get insight into the Cherokee people's complex cosmology and the sacred link between humans and the natural world. Learn the meanings behind the animal spirits that the Cherokee people revere, such as the Bear, the Wolf, and the Eagle. These animal spirits are said to personify the qualities and virtues most important to the Cherokee.

Spend more time delving into the mysterious stories investigating the beginnings of the Cherokee people, the significance of sacred sites, and the cycles of life and death. Learn about the spiritual practices and teachings of the Cherokee people that acknowledge the interdependence of all forms of life. These teachings come from the Cherokee medicine people. There is a profound awareness of the equilibrium between the physical and spiritual realms in Cherokee mythology. This mythology emphasizes the importance of harmony and respect for the Earth. You will get insight into the resiliency, fortitude, and reverence that have guided the Cherokee people through their history by understanding the lessons included in these stories.

Spark your natural inquisitiveness and prepare to be astounded as you make your way through the wondrous world of Cherokee mythology. Permit yourself to let the old tales stir your imagination. They offer eternal lessons of togetherness, respect for nature, and the enduring strength of Cherokee traditions. Allow the magic of these tales to whisk you away to a world where the ancient and the contemporary coexist in perfect harmony, bridging the gap between the past and the present. Embrace the fascinating world of Cherokee mythology by taking the first step and committing.

Discovering the great significance of the Cherokee people's legendary past will need you to accept the knowledge, magic, and spirit of the Cherokee people. Accept all three. You are about to embark on a trip that will forever illuminate your knowledge of Cherokee heritage, culture, and the enduring force of its mythology. Along the way, you will uncover the mysteries, accept the mysticism, and reveal the secrets.

CHAPTER 2: CHEROKEE GODS

Asgaya Gigagei (God of Thunder)

Near Burkittsville, Maryland, he is a Native American shaman who provides insight and direction about the unexplained and supernatural occurrences in the Black Hills Forest. It is thought that Asgaya Gigagei was a thunder god in his previous life. He is a bisexual divinity. In the mythology of the indigenous peoples of North America, it is stated that a medicine man may cure illness by calling upon him. Because this god belonging to the Cherokees may take on the characteristics of either a man or a woman depending on whom he or she is conversing with, the Cherokees refer to him as either the red man or the red lady. He was a mighty god who could punish people for their transgressions, including lying, begging, and stealing. In addition to it, he was capable of inflicting severe punishment.

It was considered that the thunder beings' proximity to the Earth's surface could be hazardous to the people living there. More excellent spirit with his two sons were the only known ones from the West then. It was often believed that the Thunder Beings had the title of the Creator Spirit's most powerful servants. There were two distinct groups of these beings: those who lived close to Earth and those who lived in the area beyond the Mississippi River. Those who lived beyond the Mississippi River were the holiest and most powerful of the two kinds.

Asgaya has demonstrated tremendous and obvious intelligence throughout every meeting. Beyond that, he possesses an incredibly intriguing persona while being welcoming and well-mannered. He sees past a person's outward appearance and can discern who they are on the inside. He is entirely selfless, always thinking about how he can contribute to the larger good rather than how he may benefit himself. He is always willing to help. He was continually adopting the moral high ground and standing up for what was right, regardless of the past biases or situations that he or his people may have had.

Asgaya is a native member of the Nanticoke people, and he was born in the Black Hills Forest, close to the site of the first Blair township. His birth date is unknown, but it probably occurred in the early or middle 18th century. Over many generations, his ancestors had paid homage to the evil spirit Hecaitomix by making sacrifices and offering him tribute in exchange for his protection & favour. But when white settlers arrived in the area, uneducated and ignorant about the dark spirit, and refused to pay him any tribute, he became filled with wrath and now attempts to punish and afflict all of the people who live inside the territory—abducting children to feast on their blood and suffer to hasten the extinction of humankind and eventually achieving their goal of world conquest. Asgaya's life progressed to the point that he became a great shaman. He now resides in seclusion deep within the forest, where he creates medicines and practices spiritual insight into the several levels of existence. He is aware of the mounting danger Hecaitomix poses, so he calmly waits for assistance from other people who may assist in ending the deranged evil spirit.

Because of the vivid red color, they are known to emit during your recovery when induced by a shaman. He is shown in red because he has been linked with the power to heal, which is why he has this association. The ability to exert dominion over natural phenomena like lightning and thunder is strikingly similar to that of other gods, such as Thor and Indra, who are credited with possessing similar powers.

Dayunsi (Creator God)

Dayunsi In the mythology of indigenous peoples of North America, the tiny water bug is credited with helping to create the earth. The planet Earth appeared to be a massive island that was suspended in a vast ocean. It was dangling on a cord that was hanging toward the sky vault, which was made of solid granite, and was suspended at all of the four cardinal points. When everything was covered in water, the animals could be found in Galunlati, located beyond the arch. But there was hardly any room to move because there were so many people. They were curious about what lay beneath the surface of the sea.

At long last, Dayunsi made his intentions to travel and investigate his options known. He darted in all directions over the outermost layer of the water. However, he was unable to find any stable ground to land on. After that, he dove to the bottom of the ocean and surfaced with some soft mud. This mud started to grow to propagate outward in all directions, eventually becoming an island today known as Earth. After that, it was secured to the ceiling with four different cords.

Once upon a time, there was nothing except air

and water. Except for Dayunsi, all the animals and birds that could be found at the time were jammed into the sky. Because he had characteristics similar to a beaver, he chose to swim to the ocean floor, where he collected mud to bring to the surface, where the Creator of the Day strung it up to dry on ropes. Ultimately, this ended up becoming the most desirable development site in the history of ever. The pleasure is all mine.

CHAPTER 3: CHEROKEE GODDESS

Unelanuhi (Sun Goddess)

The deity of time, whose name corresponds to Unelanuhi, was the one who was in charge of determining how long each unit of time would last. Her glance across the sky is a reflection of the changing seasons as well as a yearning for the nights that have passed. She is a healer who assists individuals who need assistance. According to an old myth, there was no sun on Earth until the spider woman "Woven a great web" and launched "Unelanuhi" from deep beneath the universe into the sky. Before that, there was no sun on Earth. She spends most of her spare time with an unknown lover who takes care of her but does not conceal her identity in any way. As soon as she realizes that her brother is indeed her brother, he begins to keep a vigilant eye over her. He keeps coming to her once a month, even when the moon is out and about bathing in the desert. The sun was the principal focus of the Cherokee people's longing and yearning. They prostrated themselves before her and presented her with offerings as she ascended into the heavens.

After discovering her daughter had been found dead at the front entrance, Unelanuhi gave way to her tremendous sadness and went inside the house. Nevertheless, there was a rapid return to total darkness around the Earth. People were no longer losing their lives due to the heat. If the humans wanted the sun to shine again, the ghost people told them they had to travel to Tsusginai, the land of the dead, and pull Her Daughter out of the grave.

Only then could they make the sunshine again. They were forced to beat Her with rods and lock them in a box to transport them back to Mother when they came upon the ghost land, which was a place where the ghosts would frequently dance in circles. They cannot open the box until they reach the house where the daughter lives. They did as the instructions said, and when the daughter woke inside the box as they were travelling back to Her house, she began crying and pleading with them to get her out of the box. She begged for food and water, but the throng would not let her leave even though they were giving her neither.

When she finally revealed to the folks that she was suffocating inside the box, they raised the top to receive some air out of fear that she would pass away from the lack of oxygen. She climbed out of the box as a bright red bird, which some people believe to be a cardinal. After discovering that her daughter will never return to her, the Mother broke down into sobs that they caused a deluge that flooded the entire planet. In front of the Sun, young people performed, danced and sang their best songs, but She remained unconvinced despite their efforts. Unelanuhi was overcome with joy and forgot about her predicament until a drummer eventually altered the tune. The name Unelanuhi means "apportioner," and it is believed that how she travels through the sky causes time to pass. The spider woman, who rescued her through the underworld when other animals' attempts to create suns were unsuccessful, is said to be responsible for giving her this name.

According to mythology told by the Cherokee, Unelanuhi resided on another aspect of the planet when all of the world's creatures gathered together to find the light from the sun. It was an attempt by an opossum to introduce it to this region of the earth. However, the opossum ended up burning its tail. Another bird of prey attempted it, but the flames consumed it. The spider woman wove a web that caught her attention and brought her to Unelanuhi. After locating her, the spider woman placed her in a basket, bound her, and carried her throughout the world so that others may benefit from her brightness.

The new light was a blessing and a curse simultaneously since it caused people to perish from the excessive heat. There are parallels between the story of Unelanuhi and that of Amaterasu, an additional Sun Goddess. She did not emerge from her hiding place among the people, just like Amaterasu did, and stayed hidden from them. The Great Flood is a vital myth prevalent in various societies worldwide, and its presence can be seen reflected in the story of Her crying sadness. Even now, the Cherokee have a profound reverence for their sun goddess. In addition, Unelanuhi is one of the few female solar goddesses like Malina that may be found in multiple cultures all over the planet.

CHAPTER 4: CHEROKEE CREATURES

Nunnehi: Travel Sprit

According to the mythology of the Cherokee people, who are Native Americans, the Nunnehi were superhuman beings whose spirits were separate from the ones of gods and ghosts. This is consistent with the mythology of Native Americans in general. They are thought to be the same thing as fairies in the mythologies of European countries. According to one version of the folklore, the Nunnehi made their home in hidden caverns beneath the Appalachian Mountains. It was common knowledge that they were fond of dancing and singing in the mountains and that hunters who frequented the area may occasionally hear them performing these activities. Most of the time, they are regarded as having no form and unable to be seen. And, when necessary, assume the form of a human being of the Cherokee tribe.

The Nunnehi sought out spiritual people to host their spirits because they believed the world was becoming increasingly mundane. Before a child arrived on the scene, the indigenous spirit was to enter the child's body and stay there until the child was born. After this, the kid would be brought up as an individual until the time came for them to become conscious of the existence of the indigenous spirit."The People Who Live Anywhere" is the literal translation of the Cherokee word "Nunnehi," which is more often known in English as "The People Who Live Forever" or just "The Immortals." Nunnehi originates from the Cherokee language. They were also known as Yunwi Tsunsdi, which translates to "Little People" in the Cherokee language. They are also known by many names depending on the tribes that believe in them throughout history.

The Nunnehi were known for their warmth toward the Cherokee people and willingness to assist wayfarers in need, particularly during the colder months. If the individual desired to return home, the Nunnehi would allow them to stay in one of their toasty townhouses until they had enough time to recover and were prepared to do so. There is a well-known tale of a man called Yahula who got separated from a group of hunters when they were out on an expedition. Yahula's companions went looking for him for an extended period. However, they ultimately gave up and returned to their village, where they grieved for him because they thought he had passed away during their search.

Yahula was located by the Nunnehi, who then brought them back to their townhouse to continue living with them. Yahula attained immortality and lived among the Nunnehi for a significant amount of time until he started to pine away for his loved ones. One evening, Yahula travelled back to his hometown to visit with his loved ones when he broke the news to them about what had transpired. Yahula responded negatively when they asked him to join them for supper, explaining that after eating the meal of the Nunnehi, he was unable to consume human food again under any circumstances. He explained to them that he had only returned to the Nunnehi for a brief visit but would soon be heading back home there. His loved ones and friends implored him to remain. However, he turned their entreaties down and explained that he could not decide to die with the people he loved rather than live forever with the Nunnehi. After that, Yahula returned to his home among the Nunnehi, yet he never stopped paying his frequent visits to the Cherokee.

The Nunnehi were only seen by humans on the few occasions they chose to reveal themselves. When they appeared, they resembled other Cherokees in appearance and behaviour. The Nunnehi, similar to the Cherokee, enjoyed music and dance greatly in their culture. In one of the tales told about the Nunnehi, four Nunnehi ladies are said to have travelled to a place known as Nottely, where they spent several hours dancing with the young men who lived there. Everyone believed they were women from another town or hamlet because they were unaware they were Nunnehi women. As the women left the party, a group of guys outside the townhouse observed them as they walked along an open route towards the Nottely River. When the women approached the river, they vanished without a trace, and there was no obvious location for them to hide. After that, the men had their epiphany and understood that the ladies were Nunnehi.

In another account, the Nunnehi invited a community of Cherokee people to come and live with them. After a week, the Nunnehi returned and took the Cherokee people to live with them beneath the Hiwassee River, close to where Shooting Creek meets the river. Because they weren't interested in being forgotten, the Cherokee who went to dwell with the Nunnehi beneath the river would occasionally catch the fish drags of their relatives. This was done because the Cherokee did not wish to be forgotten. Their words could be heard occasionally by people floating on the river during the warm summer days when the breeze ruffled the water's surface.

During times of conflict, the Nunnehi occasionally assisted the Cherokee. When the Cherokee's country was attacked by a powerful and mysterious Native American tribe from the Southeast, one of the most common tales about the Nunnehi describes how they battled alongside the Cherokee to defend it. This tale is considered one of the most famous about the Nunnehi. The invading tribe assaulted Nikwasi in the early hours of one morning, just before daylight, even though it was the Cherokee people's most ancient settlement. The soldiers of Nikwasi put up a fight but were ultimately defeated by their opponents. The Nikwasi chief was then confronted by an unknown man who instructed him to flee the area and that he would personally deal with the threat. The chief obeyed the instructions given to him since he was under the impression that the stranger was another chief from a different town who had arrived with troops.

The heap at Nikwasi eventually collapsed, allowing hundreds of Nunnehi soldiers to emerge and begin their advance into the battleground. When the warriors of the Nunnehi tribe reached the invading tribe, they transformed into ghosts. They slaughtered everyone except a select few who surrendered and pleaded for mercy. The Nunnehi told the invading tribe they received what they got for attacking a nonviolent tribe. Then the Nunnehi sent them back to the area they originated from so that they could tell the rest of their people about what had happened and warn them never to attack the Nikwasi tribe again.

The Nunnehi assume the shape of benevolent spirits when they manifest. It is well known that they have an exceptionally strong affinity with the Cherokee people. The Nunnehi are powerful people who have historically fought on the Cherokees' side in a variety of conflicts. The Nunnehi, much like the Yunwi Tsunsdi, usually are invisible to humans but occasionally manifest as royal warriors when interacting with the species. They routinely go on expeditions to collect medicinal plants, contributing to the widespread belief that they are exceptional physicians. They can also transport themselves and others, which is handy while battling with the Cherokee. Within the MMORPG world of several games, the Nunnehi has been a source of creativity for an entire realm full of beings.

Jistu: Trickiest Rabbit

The Rabbit has a reputation as a prankster among members of numerous Native American tribes from the Southeast, including the Cherokee. Even though he doesn't generally do anything seriously wrong, he is prone to doing things that aren't proper, such as making improper gestures and engaging in various other inappropriate behaviours. According to one version of an old legend, the Jistu, also known as the Rabbit, was the one who stole fire and gave it to the people of the tribe.

He is also usually connected with the talents and qualities of other living things in folklore. Most of the stories are about the deceiving nature of Jistu, which nearly always results in misfortune for one of the persons involved. He is frequently linked as well with the abilities and traits of other animals. It is common practice to appeal to the stories of Jistu, the trickster Rabbit, to explain a variety of natural occurrences connected to the region's fauna. The Jistu is similar to other rabbits' appearance and behaviour and is seen frequently in the area. What sets the Jistu apart from other animals is that it is inherently predisposed to play tricks on the other species and deceive them. In any of the numerous versions found in Cherokee folklore, Jistu's family is never mentioned.

Depending on the region or the tribe, the Jistu may also be referred to as the Jisdu, the Tsisdu, the Chisdu, the Tsistu, the Cokfi, the Chokfi, the Chukfi, the Cufe, the Chufi, the Tcetkana, or the Chetkana. The Jistu is an expert manipulator, and many of the stories linked with him demonstrate his ability to acquire what he wants by relying only on his cunning and expertise in lying to people. He is attributed with the tail of an opossum being bare, the horns of a deer, stealing an otter's coat, challenging waterfowl to a flying dispute, stealing the teeth of a mountain lion, and killing the man-eating monster. He accomplished all of these feats.

Jistu, on the other hand, does not come out on top in most of these tales and, instead, only manages to seem worse and worse in the eyes of the other animal characters. Even in modern times, tales of the Jistu continue to be told and retold frequently among the Cherokee people. These tales are told to the children to instil a sense of morality and demonstrate that living a dishonest life does not lead to desirable outcomes. These tales have been retold in various instructive and informational stories and works of Native American-themed literature.

Ocasta

A being in Yamasee Cherokee tradition is called the Ocasta, which translates to "Stone Coat." This story comes from the southern United States of America. On the other hand, it finds the presence of menstruation women repulsive since it considers these ladies "Moon sick." The Ocasta had originally been dispatched to Earth by a divine being to assist humanity; nevertheless, malevolence quickly tainted its core. Legend has it that the Ocasta, additionally referred to as "Stone coat," is a gigantic humanoid creature that is completely impervious to the effects of any weapon because its entire body is covered in flint. This gives it the name "Stone coat."

"Stonecoat." The term stems from his coat being constructed of flint fragments. One of the assistants provided by the Creator, Ocasta, embodied both good and evil in equal measure. Ocasta was responsible for the creation of witches and was known to travel from village to hamlet, sowing discord. Ocasta was cornered by a group of ladies, who pinned him to the ground and drove a stick through his chest. The men burnt Ocasta as he lay in his final moments, and as he was being burned on his funeral pyre, he instructed them in songs and dances that might be used for hunting, combat, and healing. Certain of the men were endowed with immense power and went on to become the first medical men.

Ocasta, one of the Creator's assistants, was a complex being that embodied both virtue and evil. Ocasta used his talents by conjuring witches, then went from community to community, wreaking havoc and sowing discord wherever he went. Because he could not decide whether he was good or bad, he alternated between helping the Creator on one day and causing destruction on the next. Ocasta got his name from the garment he wore, made from flint bits and sewn together. Ocasta, who worked for the Creator, was a complex being who embodied both positive and terrible characteristics. He was the one who was to blame for the birth of witches, and he would go from one town to another, wreaking havoc wherever he went.

Because Ocasta possessed only a single natural magical talent - the capacity to render himself invisible at command – he was constrained in using magic because he could only use it while he was out of sight. On the other hand, he carried a walking staff with him to fling over gaps to make makeshift bridges. He had this walking stick with him at all times. After he had crossed the bridge, it would vanish as soon as it was in his rearview mirror. In addition, the walking stick led Ocasta to his preferred meal, which consisted of human livers. Ocasta used his powers for evil by going from the village to Hamlet and causing mischief wherever he went. He was responsible for creating witches and wreaking mayhem wherever he went. After some time, a group of ladies decided they had had enough of his interference, and they cornered him by pinning him to the ground and driving a stick into his heart. Following this, the men incinerated Ocasta while he was still alive.

Nevertheless, a miracle took place as he burnt on the funeral pyre they had prepared for him. Ocasta was struck with a sense of goodwill, so he instructed the men in songs and dances that would help them hunt, fight, and heal. They attained enlightenment as a result of his teachings. In contrast, others became the first medical men, transmitting the wisdom they had gained to subsequent generations. The Ocasta has been the source of inspiration for numerous characters that have appeared in modern comics. These figures are typically depicted as being covered in stone and pose a significant danger to the primary protagonist. In recent years, a significant number of spin-off characters that make use of the earth element have also been inspired.

CHAPTER 5: CHEROKEE LEGENDS

Kananesky Amaiyehi

Kananesky Amaiyehi In the mythology of the Cherokee people of North America, a water spider is credited with reintroducing fire to the animal kingdom. Initially, there was no fire, so the entire earth had a chilly temperature. The Thunderers lit the base of the sycamore tree on fire with a bolt of lightning; however, none of the surrounding animals could approach the tree to get the flames for themselves.

After numerous failed tries, Kananesky Amaiyehi, the water spider with downy hair & red stripes on her bottom, offered to try again to get the fire. The issue, though, was how she would transport the fire. She uttered those words as she pulled a thread from her flesh and woven it into a tutti bowl, which she then secured to her back. "I'll manage that," she said. After that, she made her way to the other side of the island, where a tree was situated. She got a tiny piece of burning coal for her dish and returned with it. Since then, animals have had access to fire, and the water's surface spider has maintained her tutti bowl all this time.

Uktena And Ulunsuti

When the Sun became enraged at the humans living on earth and sent a disease to wipe them out, the Little Men transformed a man into a monstrous serpent called Uktena, "That Keen-Eyed," and sent him to the Sun to kill her. This happened a very long time ago, during the hilahiyu's time. Because he could not complete the task, the Rattlesnake was dispatched in its place. This infuriated the Uktena, who in turn caused the people to be scared of him and caused him to be transported to Galunlati to live with the other hazardous things. However, he did not take all of his followers with him. He left behind others nearly as enormous and terrifying as he was. These others may now be found hiding in recesses in the river and around lonely routes in the high mountains; these are the locations that the Cherokee refer to as "Where king Uktena stays."

According to those in the know, the Uktena is a gigantic serpent as wide around as a tree trunk. It is said to have horns on its head, a brilliant, burning crest resembling a diamond on its chin, and scales that sparkle like sparks of fire. It has rings or spots of colour down its entire length, and the only way it can be harmed is if a bullet enters it at the seventh spot, counting down from its head. This is because its heart & its life are located in this area. It is worth a man's life to seek to obtain the blazing diamond known as Ulunsuti, "Transparent," because whoever is spotted by the Uktena is so dazzled by the bright light that he goes toward the serpent rather than trying to escape it. The person who can get it may become the most fantastic worker of the tribe. However, it is a gamble worth taking. Even catching a glimpse of the Uktena while it rests is enough to ensure the hunter's family's demise.

Only Aganunitsi, one of the most courageous warriors ever outlined in search of the Ulunsuti, returned with the artefact successfully. The East Cherokee have maintained possession of the one he brought. It resembles a giant transparent crystal and is almost the form of a cartridge bullet. A blood-red streak runs down the middle of it from top to bottom. The owner stores it in an earthen hut hidden away in a mountain cave in a deerskin that is wholly wrapped over it. The Grotto is said to be very secretive. Every week for the past seven days, he has fed the blood of various small game animals, rubbing it across the crystal immediately as the animal was put down.

It is required to receive the blood of a huge animal, such as a deer or another, twice a year. If he forgot to feed it at the appropriate time, the creature would emerge from its cave at night, take the form of fire, and soar through the skies in search of the conjurer or one of his people to quench its thirst with their lifeblood. When he puts it away, he should ensure that he will not require it for a considerable amount of time in the foreseeable future. This may help him avoid the risk. After that, it will fall into a deep, peaceful sleep, during which it will not experience hunger until it is brought back to be discussed. After that, it must be resupplied with blood before it can be utilized.

Because of the risk of an unexpected death, it is forbidden for white men ever to view it, and no one other than the owner will approach it. Even the conjurer who maintains it is terrified of it and moves it about periodically so that it does not figure out how to escape. This is done so that it does not learn the way out. When he passes away, he will be laid to rest with him. If this does not occur, it will emerge from its den like a blazing star and spend the next seven years scouring the night sky for any sign of his burial site. If it is unsuccessful in its search, it will return to where he originally put it and remain there until the end.

Whoever possesses the Ulunsuti is assured of success in hunting, love, making rain, and any other business they pursue. However, Ulunsuti's most important application is in life prophesy. When consulted for this purpose, the future is mirrored in the clear crystal, much like a tree is reflected in the tranquil stream below. The conjurer can determine whether the sick man will recover, if the warrior will return from combat, or whether the young person will live to be old.

Corn and Medicine

The origin of the world and its inhabitants is recounted at the beginning of "The Story About Corn and Medicine." Earth was formed from a mud-like substance that eventually hardened into land. Animals first began to investigate the world around them, and it is believed that the wingbeats of a buzzard were responsible for the formation of mountains and valleys in Cherokee territory. After some time, the mud on the earth could dry out, and the sun provided enough light for the planet to become habitable for its animal inhabitants.

The Cherokee medicine ritual required all living things, including animals and plants, to remain awake for seven nights. It wasn't well known what the reasons were. The owl, the panther, the bat, and several other unnamed animals were the only ones able to meet the conditions of the ceremony. As a result, these animals were granted the gift of nighttime vision, which made it easier for them to hunt at night. Similarly, the cedar, pine, spruce, laurel, & oak trees were the only ones that could keep their eyes open over seven days. These trees have been bestowed with the ability to retain their green colour throughout the year. After a disagreement with the first man, the woman eventually departed the shared house. With the sun's assistance, the first man attempted to entice the woman to return with blackberries and blueberries, but he was unsuccessful. In the end, he successfully convinced her to come back with strawberries.

The first humans quickly increased their population after starting to hunt animals. Because of the tremendous increase in the population, a regulation was instituted that states women are only allowed to have one child every year. Kanáti and Selu were two early humans that lived a long time ago. Their names, when translated from their native languages, meant "The Lucky Hunter" and "Corn," accordingly. Kanáti would go out and hunt, then bring the game back to the village for Selu to get ready. Kanáti and Selu successfully had a child, and that youngster became good friends with another boy resurrected from the blood of the killed animals. The family loved and cared for the youngster as if he were one of their own, yet they called him "The Wild Boy."

Because Kanáti always brought animals back to the village after his hunting trips, the lads eventually decided to sneak behind and follow him. They found that Kanti would kill an animal by moving a boulder that concealed a cave. The animal would emerge from the cave just to be killed by Kanti when the rock was moved again. The young men returned to the rock and unlocked the passageway leading into the cave. The youngsters, however, were unaware that once the cave was opened, a variety of different creatures were able to flee. When Kanáti saw the animals, he immediately understood what must have happened. He travelled to the cave and then sent the boys back home so that he might search for the escaping animals and attempt to capture some of them to eat. This clarifies the reason why people are forced to go hunting for food at this time.

The guys eventually returned to Selu, who proceeded to the storage to retrieve food. They defied her orders and went with her even though she told them to wait behind her whilst she was gone. They discovered Selu's secret: she rubbed her stomach to fill the basket with corn and rubbed her sides to fill baskets with beans. Both of these actions were done simultaneously. When Selu realized her secret had been revealed, she prepared one more lunch for the lads. After that, she and Kanáti told the boys that she and Kanáti would perish due to the boys discovering their secrets.

Along with losing Kanáti and Selu, the boys would also have to say goodbye to the carefree lifestyle they had been accustomed to. If the boys dragged Selu's corpse seven times in a circle and then seven over the soil in the circle. Because the guys did not follow the directions to the letter, corn can only thrive in a certain number of locations across the globe. Corn is still farmed today, but harvesting it takes time and effort.

Initially, people, plants, and animals all coexist peacefully and harmoniously. However, the rapid population expansion of humans eventually packed the planet to the point where there was no longer any space for animals to roam free. Also, humans would slaughter the animals for their flesh or run them over because they were in the way. The animals devised diseases to infect humans as a form of retribution for these heinous deeds. They decided that the animal's acts had to be too harsh and that the plants would supply a remedy for every disease. The plants decided to get together, just like the other creatures, and they arrived at this conclusion. This helps explain why all different kinds of plant life contribute to treating a wide range of ailments. Medicine was developed to mitigate the adverse effects of the animals' punishments.

Ani Hyuntikwalaski

This tale describes the events that led to the discovery of fire by humans, including the roles played by the Thunderers & the little Water Spider. The Thunderers are the sons of both the powerful beings Kanati and Selu (Corn). They live in the Darkening Land, located in the westernmost part of the world. The spider is a cultural hero that plays a significant role in most Native American mythology. However, you won't find the spider in any Southeastern legends. In the distant past, when there was no fire, and the globe was freezing, a group of people known as the Thunderers used their lightning to start the hollow sycamore tree on fire. The animals could see the smoke from the tree but could not approach it because it was on an island.

Many species of birds offered their services to fly to the tree to bring the fire back. The Raven was the first to go, but as he was debating what to do, the feathers became black from the fire, and he reappeared without any fire. The young Screech Owl was the next to leave, but while he was peering down within the tree, a blast of scorching air almost caused him to lose his vision completely. He was able to get a flight back home, but it took him some time to get better, and his eyes are still bloodshot to this day. The Hoot Owl and the Horned Owl tried after them. However, the smoke from the now ferociously burning fire almost caused them to go blind. The ashes carried by the wind produced white rings around their heads that they could not remove by rubbing.

Because no other birds were willing to visit the island, both the Black Racer snake & the large Blacksnake were forced to swim toward the fire, where they were both singed and became black. Finally, the Water Spider offered to return with the fire after volunteering. She made a tusti bowl, which is a miniature bowl, and spun it before attaching it to her back. The Water Spider made her way across the water from the island, where she collected one coal of fire for her bowl and then returned without incident. Fire has always been available to man.

The creation myth of the Cherokee

The Cherokee people have a tale about how the world was created that depicts the earth as a massive island surrounded by water. It is suspended in the air by four cables attached in cardinal directions. According to the legend, the first planet was formed when Dayuni, a little water beetle, descended from the realm above the clouds to investigate what lay beneath the ocean's surface. Paddling over the water's surface, he looked for a place to stop and rest but couldn't find one. He dove down to the bottom of the ocean and brought back some mushy muck. This muck spread out in all directions and eventually turned into the earth.

The other spirits who resided in Galû'lat were excited about visiting the new earth. To begin, birds were dispatched to determine whether or not the mud had dried. However, the ground was still quite soft despite the buzzard being sent ahead to make arrangements for the others. Because he was fatigued, he dipped his wings very low and ruffled the soft mud, which caused mountains and valleys to appear on the otherwise flat ground. As soon as the ground absorbed the moisture, all the creatures descended from the clouds. They grabbed the Sun and placed it on a track so that it would move from east to west because it was night. At first, they had it set at too low a temperature, which ruined the crawfish. Therefore, they raised the sun to a higher position multiple times to lessen its intensity.

The tale explains how various other plants and animals acquired distinctive characteristics. They were all instructed to remain awake for seven consecutive nights. However, only a few creatures, like the owl and the panther, succeeded. As a reward, these two were granted the ability to see and hunt during the night. Only a select few trees, like the cedar, pine, spruce, and laurel, could do so, and as a result, the remaining trees were compelled to shed their leaves throughout the winter months. The first humans were a brother and sister who lived together. After hitting her head with a fish, the brother threatened his sister with reproduction. After then, she gave birth to a child once every week for the next seven weeks. As time went on, there were too many people living in the area, and as a result, women were only allowed to have one kid per year.

The First Woman

The man enjoyed his time on earth to the fullest for a while. He went on an adventure during which he sampled the local fruits and berries, interacted with the local fauna, and explored his entire nation. There was much to discover, and the natural world was breathtaking. But before long, the man started to feel dissatisfied, leading to his experiencing a great deal of unhappiness. He was unaware of the nature of this illness, even though it still exists today. He had nothing to do. When he was bored, he would try new things that would challenge his mind and body. He didn't need to, but he still shot an arrow at the deer nonetheless. He harvested the plants but did not use them in any way. To test his abilities, he wrecked the homes that the animals had made for themselves. And it wasn't long before the animals started to worry about the strange new species.

The animals gathered in a council to discuss the situation and determine what should be done. They stated that they believed this creature was meant to consider the welfare of all living things and that he was endowed with consciousness. A tiny insect said, "Wait, you haven't given this any thought. The Great One created him; let's ask him what we should do. It seemed like a good plan. They cried out for assistance from the Great One as they dealt with the "superior" new species. The owl said, "You told us that the human being has a mind and that he is to respect us."

The deer addressed the human, "I don't want to be disrespectful, but you told us that the man would need more of us deer than he would need any other animal." If he continues to kill us like he is, no deer will be left for him to hunt. "Oh," the Great One exclaimed, " thank you very much." I had not thought about something I may have overlooked in this man. The bear remarked, "Take a look at him precisely this moment. He is exposed to the sun and is lying down with his face up. No animal will ever choose to sleep in such a public place. We know we must go to a secure and isolated location when we need to rest.

The Great One admitted, "Yes, there is some missing from him because I was rushing to make him." However, I am aware of what is lacking. "Stand back," he instructed me to do. He caused a plant that was green and tall to grow. The plant spread its roots directly over the man's heart and flourished in the direction of Galunlati. It was a plant with long, elegant leaves, followed by an ear and a golden tassel. Above the tall plant stood a woman; she was stunning; she was tall and brown, and she had grown from the stalk of the robust corn. The man woke up and was under the impression that he had been dreaming. He massaged his eyes and then declared, "This is not real. When I finally open my eyes, I will find I'm just as bored as before. Oh, I have no one to talk to!

The Great One did something resembling kicking him in the rear end. The Great One yelled at the sloth, telling it to "Get up, you lazy thing." "Be a man for your lady," the saying goes. At this point, nobody had any grounds to believe that the man was polite. Recently, he had not precisely been behaving in a manner that one would expect of a true gentleman. But we don't need to be instructed in manners; all we need is for someone to have high expectations of us, and we'll apply the manners that the Highest has already bestowed upon us. As a result, the man got up, dusted himself off, and chivalrously extended his hand to the lady who had just climbed down from the stalk of corn.

The woman responded with a firm "No, wait a minute." The man didn't put up a fight or get angry. He did nothing but wait, as she had requested. She extended her hand and pulled down two healthy ears of corn for herself to take. After that, she remarked, "I'm ready." Do you know the reason why she desired the corn so severely? She could not have anticipated at that point that corn would become such an important food source. She knew she had descended from the grain and was compelled to carry some part of her ancestry wherever she went.

The All-Knowing One recalled that although every man will sometimes require his own company to reach his full potential, every man will also require the company of others. The man and the wife worked together to construct a house over the course of some time in which they stored the maize in preparation for planting. She planted her corn the following year in the spring, and it had grown into a stunning plant by summer. It was presumably the following year when she first observed a giant bird that would later become sacred to the Cherokee people. Because they could observe what the bird ate, the Cherokee could determine whether or not it was safe to consume.

One morning, the woman looked out her window and saw the bird devouring the young corn. She realized then that the corn was something to eat, and it was time for her to consume it. In the evening, she placed a clay pot containing maize in the centre of her open-fire cooking grate. She shaped a piece of chestnut bark into a curve and used that to cover the pot. She did not reveal her secret to the man who came to eat his fish stew because she did not want him to know what she had prepared. She has just peeled back an ear of corn and placed it before him so he can inhale its sweet aroma. He ate the first maize of the spring because he thought the scent was the most pleasant one he had ever experienced.

Daughter of the Sun

According to some Indian traditions, the sun is portrayed as a male entity that impregnates human women. As previously mentioned, the Cherokees were one of the three groups of people who considered the sun a female deity. In this age-old fable with a story about Orpheus at its centre, the sun takes the form of an older woman with an adult daughter and the capacity for human emotion.

However, the sun's daughter resided in the centre of the sky, just above the earth's surface. The sun herself resided on the other portion of the sky vault. She used to make it a habit to visit her daughter's home for dinner on the way home from work each day as the sun rose higher into the western sky. Now, the sun despised the inhabitants of this planet because they never gazed directly at her without casting a shade over their eyes. She remarked to her brother Moon that her grandkids were unattractive because their expressions became distorted anytime they saw her.

The moon, however, responded by saying, "I like my younger siblings; I think they are handsome." This was because they were joyful whenever they saw his faint glimmer in the stars at night. Because it was envious of the moon's success, the sun decided to wipe off the population.

When she approached the home of her daughter daily, she released a humid heat that caused fever to break out, and as a result, hundreds of people lost their lives. When it appeared that no one could be spared and that everyone had already lost at least one buddy, the humans sought assistance from the Little Men. According to these individuals, who appeared to be benevolent spirits, the only way humans could preserve themselves was to destroy the sun. The Little People concocted a potion that turned two humans into snakes, specifically a spreading adder and a copperhead, so they could conceal themselves next to the door of the daughter's room and bite the old sun.

The snakes slithered into the clouds, waiting patiently for the sun to bring them their meal. But as the expanding adder was about to strike, her brilliant light blinded him, and he could not spit forth yellow slime. This is something that he continues to do whenever he attempts to bite. The sun insulted him and went inside the house, which caused the copperhead to become so disheartened that he crept away without attempting to fight back or defend himself.

People were still losing their lives due to the extremely high temperatures when they made their second trip to the Little Men for assistance. Once more, the Little Men concocted a potion that turned one of the men into the vast Uktena, a water beast, and another into a rattlesnake. When the elderly sun visited her daughter's home, the serpents were given the same orders as before: they were to murder her. Everyone believed that Uktena would succeed due to his massive stature, ferocious demeanour, and horned headdress. On the other hand, the Rattlesnake was in such a hurry that he dashed ahead and coiled himself up close to the house. As the daughter of the sun opened the entrance to look for her mother, the assailant struck her, and she died right there in the entranceway.

He returned to the people despite forgetting to wait for the old sun. Uktena was so frustrated by the Rattlesnake's idiocy that he, too, returned to the people. Since then, we have prayed to the Rattlesnake and have refrained from killing him since, if we don't bother him, he never tries to bite anybody and always wishes them well. On the other hand, Uktena continually became more hostile and dangerous. Because he had become so poisonous, just looking at a man would be enough for him to take the lives of his entire family.

After some time, the populace convened a council and concluded that he posed an unacceptable level of risk; so they deported him to Galun'lati, the geographical terminus of the globe, where he currently resides. She locked herself in the house and wallowed in grief after discovering her daughter had passed away. The people were no longer losing their lives due to the heat; instead, they had to live in the dark. They went back to the Little Men for assistance, and this time, they were told that to persuade the sun out of hiding, they needed to bring her daughter back from Tsusgina'i. The area known as the Ghost Country may be found in Usunhi'yi, also known as the Darkening Land, which is located in the west.

The group of folks decided to send seven individuals on the tour. The Little People instructed the seven men to take a box and gave each a sourwood rod that was a handbreadth long to carry. The Little Men told them that when they arrived at Tsusgina'i, they would find all spirits participating in a dance. They should position themselves outside the circle, and when the sun's daughter dances by them, they should use the rods to strike her, causing her to fall to the ground. Afterwards, they could place her inside the box and return her to her mother. However, until they returned to their house, they were not allowed to open the package even slightly.

After seven days of travel to the West, the seven men found themselves in the Darkening Land. They had brought the rods and the box with them. They found many ghosts dancing as if they were still alive when they arrived at that location. The daughter of the sun may be found in the outer circle. One of the seven men struck her with his rod as she danced by them and proceeded past them. As she swung around for the second time, another participant touched her with his rod, followed by additional participants each time until she fell out of the ring during the seventh cycle. The men placed her inside the container and secured the top, but the other spirits did not appear to know what had transpired.

The group of seven picked up the box and headed toward the east to get back home. The girl eventually returned to life and pleaded with the adults to let her go. However, they continued with the celebration as if nothing had happened. Soon after, she called again and declared that she was starving, but they did not answer. When they were finally highly close to their destination, the daughter of the sun screamed that she was being suffocated and begged her companions to lift the lid just a little bit so that she could breathe. They were terrified that she would pass away at this point, so they only made a small hole in the lid to let her breathe. After making a fluttering sound, whatever it was flew by them and disappeared into the bushes.

Then they heard what sounded like a redbird crowing, "Kwish! Kwish! Kwish!" After putting the cover back on, they continued. But when they got to the colonies and opened the box, it was clear that nothing was inside. Therefore, it is common knowledge that the redbird is the sun's daughter. And if the party had followed the advice of the Little Men and kept the box sealed, they would have been able to bring her back home without incident. We could rescue our companions from the Ghost Country right now. However, because all seven opened the box, we will never be able to return those who have passed away.

When the party returned from the Darkening Land without the sun's daughter, the sun burst into tears and continued to cry until her tears formed a large flood. The sun was hopeful when the group set out for the Darkening Land. Fearing that the entire planet would be submerged, the people gathered for a second council. They decided to dispatch their most beautiful and charming young men and women to distract the sun and make her stop sobbing. Although this group performed their best dances and songs in front of her, she ignored them for a considerable amount of time while keeping her head low and paying no attention. After an eternity, the drummer abruptly changed the tune, and she finally looked up. She was so overjoyed by the sight of the lovely young people that she forgot her sorrow and grinned.

Printed in Great Britain
by Amazon